Amazing Young People

MALALA YOUSAFZAI

Martha London

DiscoverRoo
An Imprint of Pop!
popbooksonline.com

abdobooks.com

Published by Pop!, a division of ABDO, PO Box 398166, Minneapolis, Minnesota 55439. Copyright © 2020 by POP, LLC. International copyrights reserved in all countries. No part of this book may be reproduced in any form without written permission from the publisher. Pop!™ is a trademark and logo of POP, LLC.

Printed in the United States of America, North Mankato, Minnesota

052019
092019

THIS BOOK CONTAINS RECYCLED MATERIALS

Cover Photo: dpa picture alliance/Alamy
Interior Photos: dpa picture alliance/Alamy, 1; Henning Kaiser/picture-alliance/dpa/AP Images, 5; Shutterstock Images, 6, 23 (top), 27, 29, 30, 31; Alexandre Meneghini/AP Images, 8; Pakistan/Reuters/Newscom, 9; Veronique de Viguerie/Getty Images News/Getty Images, 11; Sherin Zada/AP Images, 12, 22 (bottom); iStockphoto, 12–13, 14, 21, 22 (top); Pakistan Press International Photo/Newscom, 15; ISPR Xinhua News Agency/Newscom, 17; K. M. Chaudary/AP Images, 18–19; Brendan McDermid/Reuters/Newscom, 20; Mary Altaffer/AP Images, 23 (bottom); Yui Mok/AP Images, 25; Cornelius Poppe/Scanpix/AP Images, 26; Muhammed Muheisen/AP Images, 28

Editor: Brienna Rossiter
Series Designer: Sarah Taplin

Library of Congress Control Number: 2018964786

Publisher's Cataloging-in-Publication Data

Names: London, Martha, author.

Title: Malala Yousafzai / by Martha London.

Description: Minneapolis, Minnesota : Pop!, 2020 | Series: Amazing young people | Includes online resources and index.

Identifiers: ISBN 9781532163678 (lib. bdg.) | ISBN 9781644940402 (pbk.) | ISBN 9781532165115 (ebook)

Subjects: LCSH: Yousafzai, Malala, 1997- --Juvenile literature. | Social justice and education--Juvenile literature. | Youth--Political activity--Biography--Juvenile literature. | Innovators--Biography--Juvenile literature.

Classification: DDC 371.822 [B]--dc23

WELCOME TO DiscoverRoo!

Pop open this book and you'll find QR codes loaded with information, so you can learn even more!

Scan this code* and others like it while you read, or visit the website below to make this book pop!

popbooksonline.com/malala-yousafzai

*Scanning QR codes requires a web-enabled smart device with a QR code reader app and a camera.

TABLE OF CONTENTS

CHAPTER 1
SCHOOL FOR GIRLS

Malala Yousafzai is an **activist**. She

works to help girls go to school.

Malala grew up in Pakistan. In 2007, an

extremist group called the Taliban

took over part of her country.

WATCH A
VIDEO HERE!

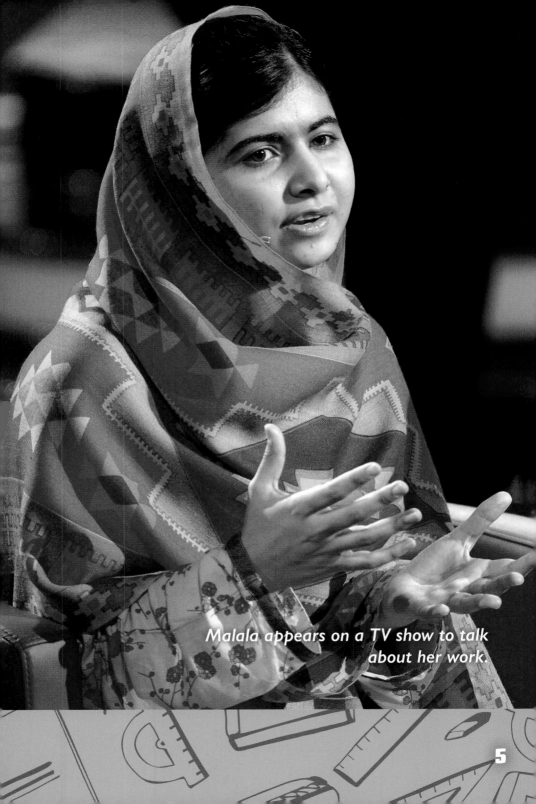

Malala appears on a TV show to talk about her work.

THE TALIBAN
IN PAKISTAN

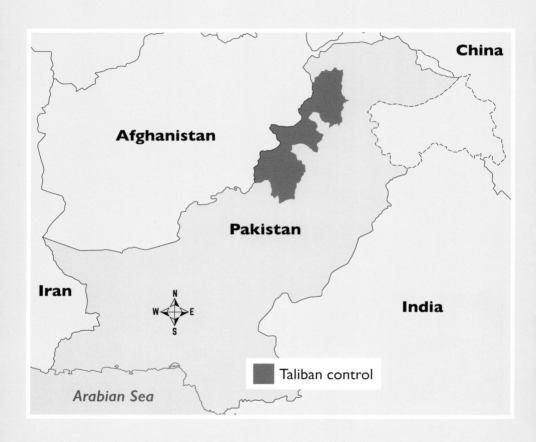

China

Afghanistan

Pakistan

Iran

India

N
W E
S

Taliban control

Arabian Sea

Taliban leaders wanted to control how people thought and behaved. They made many rules. Rules for girls and women were especially strict. If people didn't follow the rules, Taliban soldiers killed them. The Taliban also closed or bombed schools for girls. Many people were afraid.

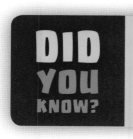

DID YOU KNOW? Some of the Taliban's rules said people could not watch TV or listen to music.

Despite the danger, Malala spoke out. She said the Taliban's actions were wrong. She said girls had a right to be educated. Her brave actions got the attention of people all over the world.

Malala's speeches told people around the world about life under Taliban control.

DID YOU KNOW?

Malala gave her first speech when she was 11 years old.

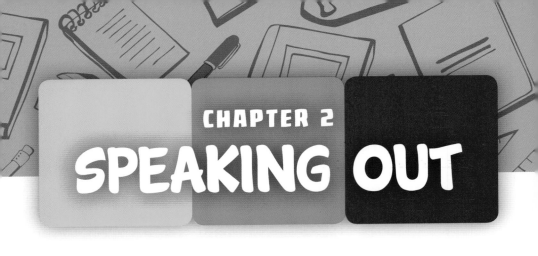

CHAPTER 2
SPEAKING OUT

Malala Yousafzai was born on July 12, 1997. She lived in Pakistan's Swat Valley. Her father was a teacher. She attended his school. In 2007, the Taliban took over. They began forcing schools to close.

LEARN MORE HERE!

An 11-year-old Malala sits in her home in Pakistan.

Children stand near the ruins of their school in Swat Valley after the Taliban destroyed it.

In 2008, Malala started giving

speeches to **protest** the Taliban's

actions. She also wrote a blog. For three

months, she described life under Taliban

control. People from many countries

read her posts.

By the end of 2009, Malala was famous. Her speeches and interviews appeared on TV around the world. Malala knew the Taliban might try to hurt her. But she continued to speak and attend school.

Malala talked about the power of learning and sharing ideas.

Pakistan's leader gives Malala an award for her work in December 2011.

CHAPTER 3
NOT SILENCED

On October 9, 2012, Taliban soldiers
stopped Malala's bus on the way home
from school. They shot Malala in the
head. They also shot two of her friends.
The girls survived. But Malala was badly

COMPLETE AN
ACTIVITY HERE!

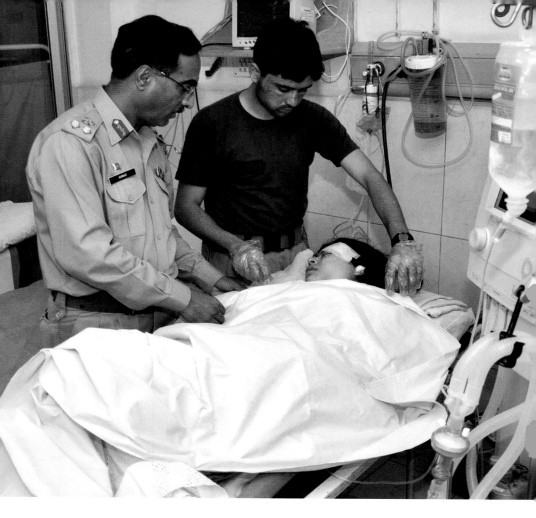

Doctors care for Malala after Taliban soldiers shot her.

hurt. Doctors rushed her to a hospital in

England. Even so, she nearly died.

News of the attack spread around

the world. Many people were horrified.

They began demanding change. Soon

Many people showed support for Malala by lighting candles and saying prayers.

after, Pakistan passed a law to help more

children go to school. And slowly, Malala

began to recover.

Malala speaks to the United Nations in July 2013.

In 2013, Malala attended a meeting

of the **United Nations**. She gave a

speech to many world leaders. She said

the Taliban tried to create silence and

fear. But she would keep fighting for girls'

rights to **equality** and education.

*The United Nations flag represents the
group's work for world peace.*

DID YOU KNOW?

**The speech took place on
Malala's 16th birthday.**

TIMELINE

1997
Malala Yousafzai is born in Swat Valley, Pakistan, on July 12.

2008
Malala gives her first speech against the Taliban.

2012
Malala is badly injured by a Taliban shooter.

2014
Malala wins the Nobel Peace Prize.

2013
Malala gives a speech to 500 world leaders at a United Nations gathering.

2017
Malala begins attending Oxford University in England.

CHAPTER 4
WORLDWIDE IMPACT

It wasn't safe for Malala to go back to Pakistan. So she and her family stayed in England. Malala attended school there. She also kept speaking out. She wanted to help children in other countries too.

LEARN MORE HERE!

Malala meets Queen Elizabeth II of England in October 2013.

DID YOU KNOW?

Malala has two younger brothers. Their names are Khushal and Atal.

Malala displays her medal after winning the Nobel Peace Prize in December 2014.

In 2014, Malala won the Nobel

Peace Prize. This award honors people

who work to make the world a better

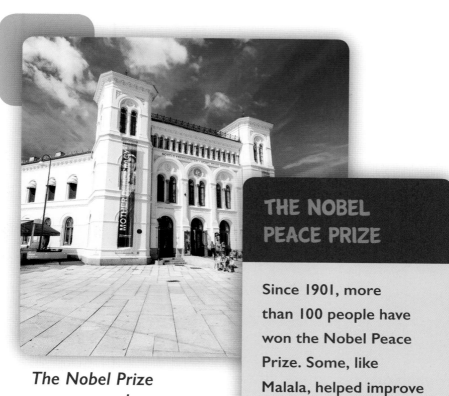

The Nobel Prize ceremony takes place at the Nobel Peace Center in Oslo, Norway.

place. Malala became the youngest person to win it. She was only 17.

THE NOBEL PEACE PRIZE

Since 1901, more than 100 people have won the Nobel Peace Prize. Some, like Malala, helped improve education. Others worked to end wars, care for sick people, or support **human rights**. Winning this prize is a great honor. Leaders such as Martin Luther King Jr. have received it in the past.

Malala and her father visit a camp in Jordan for people who have been forced to leave their homes because of war.

Today, Malala continues to work as an **activist**. She travels all around the world. She asks lawmakers to protect the rights of girls and women. She hopes that one day, every child will be able to

attend school.

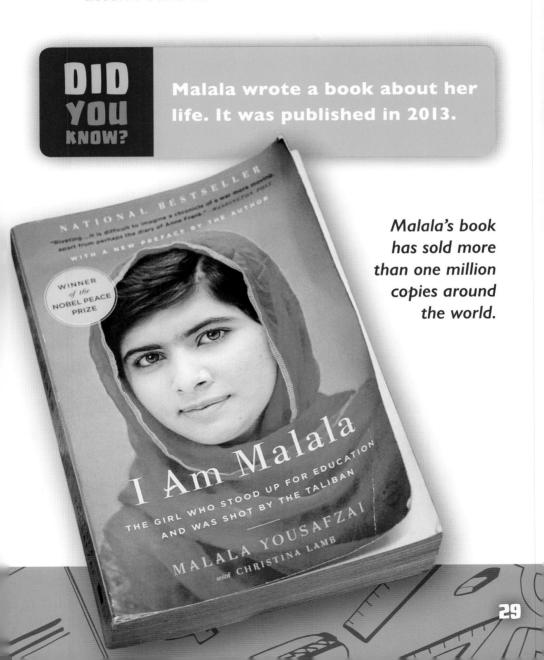

Malala's book has sold more than one million copies around the world.

NATIONAL BESTSELLER

"Riveting...It is difficult to imagine a chronicle of a war more pointed apart from perhaps the diary of Anne Frank." *WASHINGTON POST*

WITH A NEW PREFACE BY THE AUTHOR

WINNER of the NOBEL PEACE PRIZE

I Am Malala

THE GIRL WHO STOOD UP FOR EDUCATION AND WAS SHOT BY THE TALIBAN

MALALA YOUSAFZAI with CHRISTINA LAMB

MAKING CONNECTIONS

TEXT-TO-SELF

Malala spoke out to defend the rights of girls in Pakistan. Have you ever spoken out to protect someone? If so, what was it like?

TEXT-TO-TEXT

Have you read books about other activists who worked to change laws? Where did they live? What laws did they work to change?

TEXT-TO-WORLD

Malala works to help all children be able to attend school. How can education improve people's lives?

GLOSSARY

activist – a person who works to make change and protect the rights of others.

equality – treating all people the same way, not giving some more rights than others.

extremist – using fear and violence to carry out strict ideas.

human rights – rights, such as being treated fairly, that all people should have.

protest – to use words or actions to show disagreement.

United Nations – a group that works to protect the rights of people all around the world.

INDEX

 ONLINE RESOURCES

popbooksonline.com

Scan this code* and others like it while you read, or visit the website below to make this book pop!

popbooksonline.com/malala-yousafzai

*Scanning QR codes requires a web-enabled smart device with a QR code reader app and a camera.